Before You Begin. . . .

If this book has found its way into your hands, I am grateful. For the next 40 days I encourage you to embark on a journey that, for many of you, will be a new experience and perhaps a difficult one for some. Do it anyway. You will not be disappointed. The pages that follow are not intended to simply be another exercise in reading a daily scripture, followed by someone else's thoughts on the words.

My intent, my purpose, my prayer and my passion is that you will discover for yourself things about you. However you may choose to begin, do not fail to end each day's reading without writing words of your own.`

Let go of any idea of perfection. Forget sentence structure or form. Do not worry about grammar. Let the thoughts pour from within and fall on the pages. Write to yourself. Trust that the God of all Creation will hear and answer your most intimate cries, whether they be of delight, despair or devotion. There is healing in expression. I know.

If this small work is in your hands, it is by Divine Appointment.

It is my sincerest hope that you will use the pages, each one. When you have turned the last page, written the last line, and decide that you want that no one should ever see your words, then lock it up.

Finally, I would encourage you to occasionally look back, read your words, allow your own thoughts to encourage you as you understand how far you have come, how deeply you have grown, and matured. Remember the thoughts you write are about you. Do not give the pen to someone else to write what is inscribed on the tablet of your heart. Be the author of your own story. And may you be deeply blessed as you begin this new journey.

With Childlike Faith

With Childlike Faith

A 40 Day Journey

Christine Pechacek

WITH CHILDLIKE FAITH
A 40 Day Journey

For more information contact OnPoint Publishing, Harrison, MI
www.christineauthor9@gmail.com

ISBN: 0988878135
ISBN 13: 9780988878136

For My Grandchildren
Madison Christine
Noah Christopher
Zoe Elizabeth
Magdalynn Christine
Maxton Victory
May you be blessed on the journey you undertake. You are, each one, a song in my heart.

On Being Strong

Dawn had yet to break open the darkness in my quiet office as I sat with my Bible open, my journal nearby, pen in hand and my ever present cup of steaming hot coffee. The morning's devotional reading was in Joshua. I love the book of Joshua. Over and over God assures Joshua to Be strong! Be courageous! Fight the battle and win! I was feeling feisty on this quiet morning as I pondered the words in Joshua.

"Have I not commanded you: be strong and courageous? Do not be afraid or discouraged, for the Lord your God is with you wherever you go" (Joshua 1:9). As I meditated on that particular scripture, some old battles came to mind, memories of past injuries, too many still fresh and painful; so real that, like an abscessed tooth you feel compelled to bite down on, the slightest touch brought immediate, intense pain. It seemed I could never escape the pus-filled sac of poison. Once again I resigned myself that for all my life I was forced to live with an infection I neither wanted nor had caused. It made me angry all over again.

And the fact that the memory made me angry, made me angry.

"Why Lord?" The cry came up from my soul, and filled the empty space in my silent sanctuary. For what seemed the millionth time, I cried out the question to God.

And for the one-million and one time I drew in my breath to settle the pounding of my heart and gain control over the panic threatening to rise up.

Memories. I hated them. Names and faces, times and places, flew across my vision like a cruel ticker-tape parade. Closing my eyes did no good.

Forcing my gaze back to the Book of Joshua, I again read the Lord's words to Joshua, *"I have given you every place where the sole of your foot treads* (Jos 1:3). . . *No one will be able to stand against you as long as you live. . .* " (v 5).

Well, here I was again. The only feet that were treading, it seemed to me, were the ones from the past. And I was covered with heel prints. If no one was able to stand against me, then why was I the one on the ground being run over?

This record was old. I hated this song but believed myself powerless to turn the thing off. Or, to do what I really wanted to do; smash it over some heads. That was the battle I wanted to fight and win. Instead, I drank my hot coffee and sat quietly.

After a few moments I got on my knees to pray and, most importantly, to listen. I wanted to hear from God. Truthfully, I expected nothing to change in the memory-fiasco area. Resignation had become my closest companion. It is what it is, as my friend was fond of saying. One more heel imprint to my face. Each day I chose not to be a victim; however, the little foxes refused to heed my choice.

In the quiet of this morning one word came to me. Birdcage. That was it. Birdcage. A clear picture of a birdcage came to mind. As I contemplated the whole picture, I envisioned birds flitting within the confines of the wires that made up the cage, wings flopping, chirping, tweeting; desperate little birds attempting to soar only to thrust against their cage prison, frustrated, angry even, panicking to be free. They were all helpless to fly up and away. The cage I saw in my mind was locked. The birds wanted to be gone, soar up and away, but the cage held them firmly within the wire prison.

Birds confined to a cage do more than chirp, tweet and flit around. They drop feces in the bottom of the cage. Each day the caretakers of the bird's home must take out dirty, wet newspapers from the cage bottom and replace them with new fresh papers so the birds can drop more feces onto the clean papers. All in all, a disgusting picture. And a job I did not want to do. In fact, I would refuse to do it. Aside from the noise of caged birds and the filth of cage bottoms, I thought it cruel to imprison the birds. Let them fly free! That is what they are meant to do. The entire focus suddenly changed as I knelt day dreaming about a bird cage and noisy, trapped birds.

That bird cage was me. It was locked and loaded. Every one of those clamoring birds was a memory. I saw the faces of too many ugly memories flying within the confines of the cage, screaming. I realized they were screaming to get out, to fly away from me, not at me. Not one of the birds wanted to stay caged. And each trapped bird was dropping feces on my head.

In my mind, I unlocked that crowded cage. And every nasty, noisy feces-dropping bird flew away. I watched as a vision of a multitude of trapped memories flew up and far away until they were gone. Free.

It was not the last or only time I have had to unlock the cage. But that is okay. I understand that it is my cage to unlock, open up and empty out.

—~—

The area of a birdcage may be small compared to the land Joshua was given to conquer but it is no less vital and valuable. It is mine. And no bird, no memory, has the right to stay and drop feces in my land because God has given it to me. And that makes it all the more precious.

I now own a lovely birdcage that sits in my office as a reminder. It is always unlocked. And it is empty. I keep it clean by tending it carefully and watchfully. I tend to it by reading God's Word, by prayer and meditating on the Word of God. That is what I hope these pages will encourage you to do.

There is no guarantee that those nasty, noisy, feces-dropping birds will not try to fly back and make a home, but you can find strategies to keep your cage clean and well-tended. And it may very well be that you have to do it one bird at a time. It is a battle. Never underestimate the strength and determination of the enemy to destroy your soul and spirit. But it is your soul and your spirit, not the enemy's. Never forget that. Never. And the Lord God Almighty is your keeper. He is mighty to do battle.

Set your foot on your land. What that land is, only you can know. I make no claim as to how, when, where or what it looks like or should look like for you. That picture is yours to draw. But do not give the pen to someone else. And keep the key to your birdcage on your own key ring. There are places only you know and that is as it should be.

Understand too, that one of the birds flying away may be one you believe you want to keep caged. That one just might be the one dropping the most feces on your head. Let it go.

Begin today. And never cede the land God has given you. Be strong. Be courageous. God is with you O Mighty Woman of God!

Day 1

"Now the Lord said to Abram, 'Go from your country and your kindred and your father's house to the land that I will show you. I will make of you a great nation, and I will bless you, and make your name great, so that you will be a blessing"

(Gen 12:1-2).

Abraham's directive from God was clear and precise. God gave the order for Abram to go out from what he knew into what was, so far, known only to God. Scripture tells us, *"So Abram went, as the Lord had told him. . .* (v. 4). He packed up all he had, gathered his family and began a journey. He obeyed God.

There comes a time in our spiritual lives when we do know what God would have us do but because it is easier to remain where we are, we choose to do nothing. God will require obedience in a thing you have settled into because it is comfortable. It is easier to do the usual, the routine, or the safer course and never attempt the untried or the frighteningly new. Do you find it easier to say no, I will remain here in this place. I will not go out into the new, the untried.

God will require that you do go out. You must step out where He bids you go. We tend to believe all the new places are dramatic and far from our safe spots, far from home perhaps. But look closely. Is God calling you to reach out and make a new friend? Do you need to write that letter? Perhaps you are being called upon to venture out of your comfort zone that in reality has become a prison and join a new venture.

We are wired for the safe and comfortable. God calls us to Him, not to things or people but to Himself. Let the call lead you where He shows you. You will be safe. Perhaps not comfortable, but safe. Comfortable can become a strangle-hold before we realize that it is difficult to breath and unless we move, we will suffocate.

Father, You know the way that I take and although the unknown frightens me, I know You. I understand that You are Lord of All and that You see what I do not see, what I cannot see. Take my hand Lord and lead me to the place where You are. Amen

Take some time today to write out your fears. List them before the Holy Spirit. Be specific. Then lay out the list to the Lord. Pray over your list. Tell God exactly what frightens you, what you are most afraid of doing or attempting.

Day 2

"Zerubbabel's hands have laid the foundation of this house, and his hands will complete it. Then you will know that the Lord of Hosts has sent me to you. For who scorns the day of small things? These seven eyes of the Lord, which scan throughout the whole earth, will rejoice when they see the plumb line in Zerubbabel's hand."

(Zechariah 4: 9-10)

A plumb line is the tiny string covered by chalk with a weight or plumb bob at one end used to determine verticality. As a girl I watched my carpenter father use a plumb line on the new, uncut pieces of lumber. It seemed a small step in what was to be a large building project. But this tiny step determined the end. The first step, however seemingly insignificant, makes future steps resolute. It is to our own great peril, that the small things are ignored.

Today as I was on my run, I noticed a penny on the ground. I stooped over to pick it up. I often hear people say that they never bother picking up pennies on the ground. Pennies are not worth stooping for, the world needs to get rid of the penny, or, pennies cannot buy anything of value or worth. God's Word, like the coins around us is tragically, for many, counted as small morsels. People want the giant things of God's Word, the astounding miracles, not the penny shows. And so, the tiny, shimmering beauty of the small coin is passed over. Too busy and too proud to stoop over and pick up the small words, instead, it's a race to the loud, astounding display.

I save pennies. And each time I go to the store and open my wallet to pay for my purchase, I see in my coin purse are the pennies I took the time to stoop over and pick up. God's Word is the same. I read and meditate over the Word, never failing to pause, look closer, look up, look down and find the value and love for my world. Like the lone penny on the ground, that scripture, that word of the Lord is precisely what I need. It is the coin that sustains me, brings peace and hope. So I never pass the chance to pick up the pennies in God's Word. They are just what I need. At the perfect time, I can reach inside and grab hold of the coin that sustains.

Father, today I will cherish the small coins in your Word, knowing that each one is of great worth and inestimable value. Let the small beginnings be the plumb line I most need for my day, to set me on the course you have planned for me. And Lord Jehovah, fix my eyes to see the tiny coins of your living word. Amen.

Ask the Lord to show you a small treasure today, be it in His Word, or in some way throughout your day. Commit to the Lord that today you will search for, and find, the treasure He has reserved especially for you on this day.

Day 3

"Be careful to make everything according to the model of them you have been shown on the mountain."

(Exodus 25:40)

In Exodus 25:40 and again in Exodus 27:8, the Lord emphatically told Moses to be careful to do all according to the plan he received on the mountain. The mountain—a place of solitude, a place of prayer and worship, a place Moses went to be alone with God. After Paul's conversion on the Damascus road and his meeting with Ananias, Paul went away, alone. *"Immediately I conferred not with flesh and blood; neither went I up to Jerusalem to them which were apostles before me; but I went away into Arabia"* (Gal 1:16-17.) Paul went to confer with the Holy Spirit. His conversion was a complete change. He was emptied of the former Paul and became a new man in Christ. It follows then, that Paul had some things to learn and un-learn.

Paul and Moses teach a great truth; that, all I need to learn, I learn at the feet of Christ and on His Mountain, alone with Him. F.B. Meyer writes, "[t]he anointing of the Holy Spirit makes human teaching unnecessary because it teaches all things." Does that mean that I ignore learning? Not at all. But the Spirit's teaching is the richest and forms the basis for all other learning. In being alone with the Lord, I come to understand intimately that *"God's ways are not [my] ways and His thoughts are not [my] thoughts"* (Is 55:8).

As I approach the great mountain of God, I pray God will hold my hand, walk me through the labyrinth of learning, training and understanding of His ways. God has every right and my permission to stop me along the pathway whenever and wherever He chooses that I may see as He sees, feel as He feels.

It is during the time on the mountain, traveling with God, that God's vision for a life is revealed. And not surprisingly, it is so often different than what our focus would be.

Lord God, I desire to be alone with you, to hear your voice, to see your face, to be made what you have planned for me. And not just today, but a part of my every day. I will come to the Mountain and wait for You. And I will return again and again, day after day for you alone have the words of Life. Amen.

Today take time to tell the Lord your mountain. Share with the Lord of All Creation, your sorrow, your pain as you face this day. Be specific. God desires to hear from you and for you to share the depth of your heart with Him.

Day 4

"[Abraham] believed in God, who gives life to the dead and calls things into existence that do not exist. . . Against hope, with hope he believed. . .He considered his own body to be already dead. . .and the deadness of Sarah's womb. . .

(Romans 4:16-21).

Oswald Chambers wrote about the necessity of having our own "white funeral". Dead to ourselves, our own aspirations, our dreams, our goals and alive to the one and only reality, found in Jesus Christ's death and resurrection. How easy to speak the words. The phrase becomes one of sentiment, stripped of all meaning, uttered in emotion, with little or no consideration of the cost not only to self but to those whom we love and hold dear.

Sarah's womb was in a state of *nekrosis,* deadness in the sense of human ability. Abraham did not waver in unbelief but he held steadfast to the One who calls life out of death, and brings into existence what is not. Abraham attended his own white funeral. His advanced years, Sarah's old age, and dead womb meant that the staggering promise coming from God Himself could come in no other way but by the Divine hand of the Most High God. Abraham had no human ability to make happen what God declared was coming. But, he held fast to the promise giver.

It is in the place of deadness and darkness that God calls forth life. When all human ability is gone and dead, only then will we stand in the awful light of God's glory and behold the dried up womb within come to life with the birth of God's will, His stunning plans for our lives, and watch and behold as God calls into existence those things that are not.

You may believe today that everything you hold dear is dead, in a state of *nekrosis*, but that is precisely where God begins. When our human ability is gone, we see what God and only God can do. He stands ready to bring life where we only see death.

Father God, Shadi, today I will walk with you to my white funeral and watch as my life becomes new in You. I will walk in the funeral procession rejoicing that what awaits me is the birth of more than I could ever hope to imagine or begin to accomplish on my own. Thank you. Amen.

Today give to God all the dead things in your life. Write out the things that in your eyes are in a state of *nekrosis*. Tell God that you know there is no human thing you are able to do. Be specific.

Day 5

"How long, Lord, must I call for help and you do not listen, or cry out to You about violence and You do not save? Why do You force me to look at injustice? Why do You tolerate wrongdoing?"

(Habakkuk 1:2-3)

Habakkuk cried out to God to be shown some justice. He wanted God to answer his complaint. He called to God to look for himself at the mess the world was in and only getting worse. *"How long God?"* Everything around him had gone mad. Nothing right or just was allowed to prevail it seemed. And so Habakkuk stated his case before God's court, describing in detail what was happening. And then cried out to God, *"Why are you silent. . .?"*

I understand Habakkuk's complaints. I want the world to be right. I want fairness to prevail. I want justice to be done at every turn. I want the treacherous exposed and liars revealed. My eyes are often red with tears because of hurts in my life that I had nothing to do with causing. Unfairness abounds because of the wicked. Consequences of others actions fall on me as surely as an avalanche I have no control over and rarely see coming.

And like Habakkuk, I stand at my devotional doorpost as I pray and meditate on His Word with arms folded across my chest and say to God, 'what are you going to do about this?' I want action and I want it right now. The Prophet listened then as God answered his complaint.

As God speaks, it is our call to listen to His Words. As he heard the voice of the Almighty resound, Habakkuk listened in stillness as God told him to be patient. He assured Habakkuk that He was aware of every complaint, every frustration and every unfairness in the world and Habakkuk's life. God knows what He is doing.

What goes on in this world is of no consequence in terms of my faithfulness to Jesus Christ. The world may fall and crash into the sea. All I know may be swallowed up by the terrors of life, but I am called to remain faithful in all things and in all circumstances. That is the highest calling, faithfulness to the one and only Lord God of Heaven, Jesus our Savior. And not one iota is dependent upon my outward circumstances, people or things.

O God you are the Ancient of Days. I will wait on you. I will trust you in plenty and in want, in tears and laughter, and in good times and bad. Nothing from without can destroy my love for You. You are faithful and true. I will triumph in You. You are my strength and my song. Amen.

Today take time to write a letter to the Lord. Express your sorrow and your frustrations over the wrongs you see, the unfairness you struggle with each day. Write as to a friend who has a deep love for you.

Day 6

"Am I a God who is only near"—this is the Lord's declaration—"and not a God who is far away? Can a man hide himself in secret places where I cannot see him?"—the Lord's declaration. "Do I not fill the heavens and the earth?"—the Lord's declaration"

(Jeremiah 23:23-24).

God prepares us for His service. We receive a vision or a call. God makes a declaration on a life. It is an assurance that what we desire is surely of God. The call comes from deep within and is confirmed over and over again by songs we hear, scripture we read, comments by friends or a particular message from the pulpit. We can determine and understand the call; but, we are far from equipped.

Oswald Chambers writes that it is at this point that God takes us down into a valley and batters us into shape. The valley is never one of our choosing. Jeremiah watched as the potter smashed the clay so he might begin again and make something new from the already worked clay. The familiar picture is one I return to again and again. Each time I believe I have been battered and smashed as much as is possible and survive, there comes another wham! Finally, when surely there can be no more hammering possible, the oven door opens and I am thrust into its intense heat.

"I know the plans I have for you, says the Lord. Plans to prosper you and not to harm you. Plans to give you a future and a hope" (Jer 29:11). That is the future

and hope we all desire. A future and hope found in Christ alone. Like Paul, I will rejoice in my sufferings, because I know that the Creator, Savior, King of Kings, has plans for me. His plans are a future and a hope. Nothing on this earth or in the heavenlies can compare to what Christ has planned. I cannot argue with such perfection.

Nothing is out of His control. Nothing. No enemy can come into a life that has not gone before the Throne first. I live in the here and now, on this earth; but, my life is wrapped up in the arms of the Savior and I am covered by the blood of the Lamb. My heavenly Father tells me to trust Him. His Word is full of promise, hope and examples of exactly why it's a good deal to trust Him.

It would be well if, each day, when the enemy attempts to rear the ugly head of dismay, fear, anxiety and doubt, we reply, "You need to go and talk to my Abba. I have nothing to say to you."

Father God, I sing along with those who say, 'My hope is built on nothing less that Jesus Christ and His righteousness.' I will go with the throng who enter the gates of praise and lay all that I am before you. You are my everything and I trust you. Amen.

Take some time today to write a love letter to the Lord. Express your trust in His never failing love. Allow His Word to seep into your heart and soul with the real truths of who you are and who He is to deliver you, to encourage you and to bring you peace.

Day 7

"So Moses went back to the Lord and asked, 'Lord, why have you caused trouble for this people? And why did you ever send me? Ever since I went in to Pharaoh to speak in Your name he has caused trouble. . .[t]he Lord replied to Moses, 'Now you are going to see what I will do to Pharaoh: he will let them go because of My strong hand. . ."

(Exodus 5:22-6:1).

I love the Old Testament. Its richness is beyond comprehension; which is why, when I study the Old Testament, I have a Hebrew-Greek Study Bible on my knee. To assume that the words you see on the page are all there is to the verse is to miss great blessings. We are called to study and discern God's Word. In this passage, Moses was mystified, even angry, that the Lord sent him to bring the people out in a great deliverance only to see greater trouble.

The situation Moses faced is one to which we can all relate. How often I have cried out to God. Lord, you sent me, you called me, I went, I obeyed and look at this mess. God told Moses that now the time was ripe for him and all the Israelites to see how mighty His power is to deliver. There is emphasis on the word *now.* God is telling Moses that the stage is set, the details are according to His plan and time. The glory of the Lord will shine, His power and His alone, will amaze and astound. God announced that His love for His people is so great that He waited. But NOW is the time. The word tells that the stage was set—through all the misery and hurt, not in spite of it.

Moses understands that God set it up. Pharaoh was a pawn to showcase God's love and deliverance. After every avenue failed, every escape route locked up, then God came and said, Okay, NOW. It is God and God alone who delivers. I cannot know God's mighty power to deliver unless and until my eyes are fixed upon Him, until I understand that every help of man is worthless (Ps 60:11). Man's help is vain, useless, unreal, and even destructive.

We may fight, rage, work harder, plan more and even scheme, but it is God and God alone from whence cometh our help (Ps 121). Too often we find ourselves strung out on a branch with no lifeline in sight and no hope. And like Moses, we ask God what is He doing? To which the Sovereign Lord replies, *Stand back! NOW you are going to see what I, and I alone, will do.*

Father, you are so patient with me. I cry and fight, all to no avail, and it is then and only then that I stand back, and relinquish my all to you. And I am stunned again and again by the Almighty Hand that reaches down to me and delivers. I praise you for your faithfulness to me. Amen.

Tell the Lord the details of the situation you face today. Explain to Him your sense of helplessness and fear that you will be overwhelmed. Finish by asking God specifically what He will do. Then listen and allow the quietness of the Holy Spirit to fill you as you wait upon Him.

Day 8

"Therefore, go. I am sending you to Pharaoh so that you may lead my people, the Israelites out of Egypt."

(Exodus 3:10)

God sent Moses into the fray, the danger that was Egypt. It was a deliberate decision by God. The Lord sent Moses into, not away from, the mess. Interesting. Moses was unsure. He knew he had nothing in himself with which to fight Pharaoh and his mighty forces.

That was the point. Moses was defenseless on his own. He said to God, who am I, that I should go? God's answer, "I will certainly be with you" (v.12) did not strike Moses as sufficient. Moses continued with "but. . . " Perhaps Moses, just as we, failed to hear the emphasis on the word "I". God said to Moses, "I AM THAT I AM'. When I read that scripture, I am certain I can hear the boom of God's voice come from the heavens.

So often I just doggedly keep trying to defend my reasons, I look for man's ways, some plan I can latch onto, or to see a reason for it all. The chaos and strife of life is meant to drive God's people to look to heaven and cry out for God. I ask God, who am I that I should do this thing? How can I, of all people, go straight into situations and expect results? What can I say? Who will listen to me?

"I AM hath sent me" is all I need to know for the present. The Lord Almighty, God Jehovah goes before me. The great I AM. There is a chorus that reminds us of this fact. “Who is like the Lord?” And the refrain answers the question, “There is no one. He is strong and mighty”.

God told Moses, you go. I will help you. I will use you to show Pharaoh my mighty hand. The Great I AM says the same to you and to me. Trust the Great I AM. And what is required of us? To go. Put one foot in front of the other and go. To “. . .stand firm and see the Lord’s salvation. He will provide for you today. . .the Lord will fight for you; you must be quiet” (EX 14:13-14).

Father God, you are the Great I AM. I will trust you today for that which I cannot see. Your eyes roam throughout the earth, watching and keeping. I will rest confident in the knowledge that not one hair of my head will fall but that you will see and take care. I love you O Lord. Amen.

Tell God the situation you face right now. Write out to Him the dire circumstances, the hurt and your fear that you will not survive the days ahead. Tell God who is the Pharaoh who taunts you. And ask God to show you who He is. Declare that you know God to be I AM THAT I AM.

Day 9

"Aren't two sparrows sold for a penny? Yet not one of them falls to the ground without your Father's consent. But even the hairs on your head have all been counted. Don't be afraid therefore; you are worth more than many sparrows"

(Matthew 10:29-30).

I am amazed over and over again at the awesomeness of God. It is so easy to just move along in life and not truly appreciate the immensity and majesty of the Savior. Or, to get caught up in the vastness and forget that God, the Almighty, King of Kings is personal, loving and close to our side. I appreciate that God takes the time to remind me of who He is to me, all the time, not just in church, not only when I am reading His Word, but always. Not one hair of my head falls to the ground but that He knows. His eyes watch as that single hair flutters, is caught by a slight movement or breeze, and slowly drops off my shoulder and onto the ground. His eyes behold all things, past, present and future. The thought staggers me. But more astounding and profoundly more intimate, is the knowledge that the eyes of the Almighty Creator, El Ro-ee, the God Who Sees Me, sees *me.*

We are all, as individuals, not just a mass of humanity; a part of God's created order and grandeur. God is not capricious nor is He haphazard or careless in this world that His own hands have created. This thought presses upon me and brings praise, often unbidden, from my lips. *How Great Thou Art.* I am the apple of His eye (Ps 56:8). When God looks at the palm of His nail scarred hand, He sees my name inscribed there, never to be forgotten, put aside, or ignored (Is 49:16). I am overwhelmed with the realization that I matter to God in a most intimate way that my life is forever stamped with the signature. . . JEHOVAH.

My steps are ordered by God. All my tears are captured by the nail scarred hands and gently put into a bottle (Ps 56:8). We can for a time perhaps believe that God cares little for the day-to-day things of our lives. That is a lie, of course. We all matter. Every word upon each tongue, each touch of the hand, smiles, laughter, and tears—it all matters.

O Father God, you live in me. What an incomprehensible truth. What a gift. Today make me aware of this wondrous life so freely given to me at such a great cost. I will live today with purpose and praise for so matchless a Savior. Amen

Express to God today that you want to understand that you matter to Him in a very real and personal way. Write out to God the thing that today you want to know is lovingly and personally in His care and love.

Day 10

"When Jesus saw large crowds around Him, He gave the order to go to the other side of the sea. A scribe approached Him and said, 'Teacher, I will follow you wherever You go!' Jesus told him, 'Foxes have dens and birds of the sky have nests, but the Son of Man has no place to lay His head.' 'Lord,' another of His disciples said, 'first let me go bury my father.' But Jesus told him, 'Follow me, and let the dead bury their own dead'"

(Matt 8:18;22).

Oftentimes I will do anything except follow. I want to fix what needs to be fixed before turning to follow. There is in me the desire to expose the misdeeds I see around me, I want to make right what I see as wrong, straighten what I see as crooked, and bring to tears where I believe tears should flow. Jesus tells me to follow Him. Turn away from all the cares and worries, turn from the machinations of the world that surround me and follow Jesus.

Each year when winter finally makes its appearance, when the ice and snow and cold temperatures are here for a protracted period of time, and the branches hang heavy with the weight of snow, God's power and mercy are on full display. His power changes the seasons, unbidden by man, His majesty blankets the ground with snow despite my feeble protests, and His mercy is on spectacular display.

Recently I drove a quiet, seldom used stretch of highway and pondered the stillness and quiet of the myriad number of snow-covered trees, branches laden with snow, hanging under its weight. And quietly, I listened to the Holy Spirit. *Just as the snow covers the ground bringing rest to its soil, and the branches hang heavy with the weight of my snow so they too may know rest, I bring a time of rest to all souls. Rest in Me. Springtime will come and new life will grow. Trust Me. Follow Me.*

Jesus bids us, each one, to follow Him, to rest in, and under, His majesty of strength. Take time to view the wonder of God's mighty work, not only in nature but from within. Let the dead bury their dead. Let the cares of the world care for themselves. Follow Christ to the other side of the sea. Rest in Him and wait for springtime.

Sovereign Lord, you are my resting place. I find my comfort in you as in none other. This day I will follow you to the other side of whatever sea you take me on. I will follow you wherever you lead. You are my Lord. Amen.

Take time to write out your thoughts of God's providential care for you. Reaffirm your commitment to follow the Master where He leads.

Day 11

"The blood on the houses where you are staying will be a distinguishing mark for you; when I see the blood, I will pass over you. No plague will be among you to destroy you when I strike the land of Egypt"

(EXODUS 12:13).

God was delivering His people! The final plague was coming, the Angel of Death. This awful night would be marked by the death of every first born male in every household. Every household except those of the Israelites. God's specific instruction to His people was to mark the lintel and doorposts with the blood of a sacrificial lamb. The Angel of Death saw the blood sacrifice and passed over that so marked house. The blood of the lamb marked the Israelite household as saved from the horrific death the Angel brought and inflicted on the Egyptians who had so defied the Living God.

What a promise for today. The blood of Jesus, our sacrificial Lamb marks us as saved from certain, eternal death. We walk in the robe of the righteousness of Jesus. We are saved. The plague of the terrible enemy of our souls must pass by the children of the Most High God. The enemy whispers and taunts as he passes by in our night but he may never pass through the blood of Jesus. The enemy may not enter my house, my salvation, my peace or my relationship with Jesus Christ (v23). He may snarl, scream, plan all sorts of evil against me, and threaten my very heart, but that is all he can do. I am marked with the Blood of the Lamb.

"And the Lord gave the people such favor in the Egyptians sight that they gave them what they requested. In this way, they plundered the Egyptians (v36). I am in awe of this verse. God granted such favor to His children, the Egyptians were compelled to give to them everything. It is the same favor that God bestows on His children today. It is not the favor of material goods; but, it is the profound knowledge that the enemy of our souls is plundered to the point of powerlessness. It is hubris that drives the tempter to great heights of evil. It is the blood of the Lamb that stops the advance and brings victory to His own.

Today, Lord, I will walk in the truth of Your Word. I praise You that I am covered by the Blood of the Lamb and sealed in Your love. Thank You that I walk in Your favor and that no enemy may pass through You to me. I will celebrate that victory today. Amen.

What has God delivered you from recently? It is not always the spectacular but often the less-than grand little things that would mar our soul and spirit. A bad attitude? Temptation to gossip? Write today of those things that have clamored at you. Now, record God's promises to be with you in all things and to deliver you into His care.

Day 12

"For I am the Lord, who brought you up from the Land of Egypt to be your God, so you must be holy because I am holy"

(Lev 11:44).

"For God has so constituted us that when we sin against the laws of truth, purity, and righteousness, decay immediately sets in by an inevitable law." F. B. Meyer wrote the words some one-hundred years ago. The years cannot diminish their truth but sadly, they mean as little to the world today as perhaps they did in Rev. Meyer's time.

We do not see decay on the faces around us. We cannot visualize the decay that begins in our own heart and soul when we choose the spiral of veering from God's truth. But it is there. Each step apart from the Holy Spirit makes the next one easier to take. The clamor of voices screaming to watch the profane, listen to the profanity, and to accept what we know to be untenable is a mark, a tiny cut that, while it does not bleed profusely, alerting us to some horrible infection or threaten our life, nevertheless, erodes at the life of Jesus within. Scar tissue forms, making the spot tougher, more resistant to further calling by the voice of the Savior.

We are called to be holy as He is Holy. Such holiness is not obtainable unless and until the Holy Spirit takes up residence. And God's Spirit cannot abide with sin. It is impossible for a Holy God to live with sin. He sent his only Son to die for sin that we might become one with Him. Christ's death on the cross made my way to the Father possible. I rejoice in that. I also know that when I sin, there is forgiveness through the atoning Blood. The cost was so great for the Father; and yet, He loved me so much that the price was paid. Because I am brought with such a great price, as Paul says, (I Corn 7:23), I will not knowingly become a slave of sin.

Several years ago a plastic bracelet appeared, WWJD, meaning what would Jesus do? How easily some letters on a wristband substituted for true belief that results in holy behavior. It brings the gift of eternal life, Jesus death on the cross and God's call to be holy to the level of what Dietrich Bonhoeffer termed *cheap grace.* I know what Jesus would do.

He has given me a book of great detail to read daily that I might know exactly what He will do, has done and will continue to do.

Heavenly Father, I will daily read Your Word that I may hide it in my heart that I will not sin against you. And when I do, I have an advocate, the Holy Spirit to speak on my behalf to the Father. I will draw close to you each day that I may guard against the decay of this world. Amen.

What are some of the enemies of your soul? Talk with the Father about each one and wait upon Him for the armor that will cover you for the day.

Day 13

"God is our refuge and strength, a very present help in trouble. Therefore we will not fear, though the earth be removed and though the mountain be carried into the midst of the sea. . .Be still and know that I am God; I will be exalted in the earth"

(Ps 46: 1-2, 10).

The Psalmist adjures us to quiet ourselves that we may know God. It seems more and more difficult to accomplish stillness in a world of music, television, games coming from a disembodied screen, movies and all things electronic that scream for attention. The sight and sounds of the world clamor but we are under no obligation to answer the outcry. We all have the authority to answer or ignore. The headphones do not jump up and strap themselves to unsuspecting ears.

God will not compete for our time and attention. The Lord of All does not advertise, promising the latest and greatest in order that we might opt for His offerings rather than the latest social media. While those things have their place in the hierarchy of what I know to be important, I do not put God in the line of choices. He is The Great I AM. God is God and will not abdicate His throne for any authority. In refusing to put God first, as we go on our way, too busy with what we deem to be vital and life-giving, we are the losers.

God is not diminished by our absence from His presence. The Almighty is not left alone, lamenting that we have ignored Him. God is. God remains whole and complete. He is Omnipotent, Omnipresent, and Omniscient God. As He was before time, He will never be less. God's sorrow at our absence, our frenzied coming and going as He is shut out of lives, is sorrow for what we are missing. El Ro-ee, the God who sees me, watches as we rush off, perplexed, burdened, frightened and anxious to face another day, knowing that we have left behind the protection of His Armor, the whisper of His still, small voice, and His eternal wisdom that assures me I am a child of the King of Kings. God's heart calls us so that we might find rest in His presence.

Daily time alone with the Lord is a life-line. Be assured that nothing comes into a life each day that is haphazard or capricious. Rest in the knowledge that all has gone before the Throne first and received God's stamp of approval for learning, growth, stretching and correction. We ignore God to our own peril.

Thank you Adoni Ehloheem, Lord God, that You so love me that I am called into Your very presence to fellowship with You. I will quiet myself in Your presence so I may know and be known by You. Amen.

Set aside time each day for God alone. If it is difficult, then begin with 15 minutes. The important thing is to begin. Commit to God that you will sit in His presence quietly. Record your thoughts as you sit quietly, waiting on the Holy Spirit.

Day 14

"The people cried out, 'Give us a king to judge us as all the other nations have. . .' Samuel considered their demand sinful so he prayed to the Lord. But the Lord told him, 'Listen to the people and everything they say to you. They have not rejected you; they have rejected Me as their king.'"

(I Samuel 8:5-7).

In 1 Samuel 10:35 the great prophet, Samuel, had just anointed Saul as king. He did as God commanded even though, he, Samuel, knew that in truth God was their King. His words fell on deaf ears. The people cried out to have a king like the sinful nations around them. And so Saul became their king.

It is all too easy to reject the Lord in our lives, our daily thoughts and activities. God promises us freedom, strength in times of weakness, joy in our mourning, deliverance in times of need, protection against the enemy of this world; but, instead He is ignored. The fleeting, transitory pleasures of this brief life are placed over and above the riches of all that God offers. Pleasures and foundations that cannot hope to save or deliver rise to the forefront.

In Zachariah 3:1-2, Joshua as high priest is standing before the Angel of the Lord and Satan, the lethal opponent, is standing at his right side, ready to accuse Joshua. And the Lord rebuked Satan. That is you and I. The Lord stands at our side to rebuke the enemy of our soul. What glory!

Satan stands ready every single day, every hour, to accuse all of God's children. He stands near to whisper out every failure, each time we fall short, and every moment of doubt. He is the father of lies.

The Lord, strong and mighty, stands ready to refute every lie and accusation. It is our inheritance from the Lord. God, the Almighty, has removed our filthy garments of guilt and sin (Zachariah 3:3-7). We are not left standing naked, open to ridicule and unprotected. We are dressed with holy garments, His divine indwelling. We are called to a mighty work in the Lord. He has called us to walk in His ways, keep His instructions so we may rule His house and take care of the very courts of the Lord God Almighty. What a high calling.

Lord, to whom shall I go? You are the Word of Life. You stand with me, protect me and share all things in heaven with me. Let me solemnly and with reverence put on the garments of Your Word every day. Thank you. Amen.

Write words today to the Lord of your commitment new and fresh to stand with God. Tell the Lord of your trust in His unfailing protection and guidance.

Day 15

"But we did not yield in submission to these people for even an hour, so that the truth of the gospel would remain for you"

(Galations 2:5).

Following Paul's vivid experience on the road to Damascus, he clearly did not confer with men. He did not get their opinions or takes on the matter. Paul turned from a persecutor to a missionary of all men. It was the reality of Christ and the Gospel that affected Paul's change. He remained skeptical of the voices of others and of the dangers of being led astray by false gospels.

We must guard fervently against yielding to a false truth, even for one minute. Stand firm. If the words you hear are one iota from the truth of the gospel, do not yield. Do not say to yourself that what you hear is just a little from the truth. Oh, I may not speak up to that small issue. I am able to absorb those words and still be on firm footing with the gospel. You cannot. You will not. Your foot will begin a slide from which you may never recover. One small sway with a breeze will lead to another and another, until the slight movements are barely noticeable and then you find yourself a reed shaken by the slightest breeze, tossing and turning, unstable in all your ways (James 1:8) and vulnerable to those who prey on the unstable (2Pet 2:14).

Acquiescing to half-truths, or comfortable truths, in the hopes of feeling better about ourselves, or tragically to alleviate our guilt over sin, will crash and burn every time. And it will do so with ferocity we cannot imagine.

What need do the lost have of half-truths, saving-truths? The diluted, attractive gospel of the world is attractive because it is stripped of the agony of the cross and the hell of sin. Hubris will draw crowds of the lost and then it will kill them.

Sovereign Lord, keep me alert and alive to the one and only truth of Your Word, Jesus Christ, and He crucified. Hold me accountable to every line and each word, without exception, doubting or sway. Amen.

What half-truths do you see around you? Speak truth in all things. Never allow yourself to become persuaded that a half-truth is good enough. It never is.

Day 16

"The life I now live in the flesh, I live by faith in the Son of God, who loved me and gave Himself for me. I do not set aside the grace of God; for if righteousness comes through the law, then Christ died for nothing

(Galatians 2: 20-21).

If I can do or be anything righteous or good, kind or loving on my own merit, then Christ's death was a waste. The agony of the cross was good drama, nothing more. It stands merely as a rallying point for a cause to stir me up and give me pride for a moral cause. If my words stir people to be moved to a moral happening, then what need have I or anyone else of the great salvation wrought by Jesus Christ?

It is by grace and grace alone that we are anything. We stand or fall by God's arm reaching out in compassion. Each morning a new battlefield is opened up amidst us. Our feet hit the floor and the enemy has been planning all night as we slept how best to cause our downfall. Will it be the weapon of pride, shined and honed, to remind us of our own skill in accomplishing the day? Perhaps reminding us of how bedazzled the crowds were as we stood to share our own dramatic story. Or maybe the successful career earned through our own hard work and education will be the firing shot to seduce us away from Christ and Christ alone as our strength. Possibly a swell of pride disguised as humility for the way we are able to just slide through a day in our weakened and sorrowful state.

Rejoice that we are able to do nothing without the righteousness of God. Rejoice that we can do anything and everything with His grace and righteousness. It remains a conundrum to our earth-bound thinking that we are at once nothing and yet everything. I surrender all. In my surrender, I win. I become a prisoner of the Gospel. In being a prisoner, I am free as no earthly master could make me. It is a mystery, one of such beauty and grace that our earthly selves are not able to behold its wonder. And yet, to we who embrace and believe, the mystery is no mystery at all.

Oh matchless wonder, Your majesty is beyond me. I revel in the splendor of your unimaginable wholeness. You are my God and I praise You. All my worship is in You. Bring praise from these lips for in my humanness I am speechless. Amen.

Write out for today what you will face that threatens your walk with Jesus. No issue is too small to bring before the Lord. Allow God to remind you of who He is.

Day 17

"An unguarded strength is a double weakness."

Oswald Chambers

Never for a moment think you have conquered that habit or left that former sin behind forever. The temptation lurks at your feet waiting for a more opportune time. The years since you accept Christ as your Savior may be many. You have, and now are, living a life filled with the Holy Spirit. The enemy is in your shadows waiting for the moment when, in a burst of pride, you say, *O, I would never do that again. That was my old life. Look at me now. I am beyond that sin.* And your guard begins to loosen and slip imperceptibly.

Your urgent prayers to the Lord to keep you under the shadow of the Almighty are quieter now. The realization that you are kept by the power of grace and grace alone becomes a mere whisper of truth. The moment that your mind begins to tell your heart that you are too wise for such temptations and that the devil will never reach you on that plain again because your walls are too secure, that is the moment the enemy sees that you are unguarded. His opportunity is nigh.

Remember the enemy of your soul is patient as death. With all the cunning of a serpent, he coils in a dark place, quiet, waiting to strike at that place in your wall of defense you have left wide open. It will never be the big thing, the huge gap in your defenses that you are aware is there. It will be the tiny place of strength that you have left unguarded. *I am secure in this area. The years have passed and that temptation has not called to me.* Be sure that is exactly where it will attack if left unguarded.

Daily remember you are strong only in Christ. Use the Word to secure the ramparts. Praise and sing Psalms of deliverance for a battle you are ill-equipped to fight on your own.

Then let the enemy batter his head at your wall of defense, secure in the knowledge that all hope and power is *built on nothing less than Jesus Christ and His righteousness.*

Lord, I am never out of your grace. I am saved by the blood of the Lamb and kept by your strength. Today and each day I will call upon your name to keep me and strengthen me in all ways. It is not of myself that I rest secure, it is only on the breast of the Lord where I lay my all every moment of every day. Amen.

Make a list of the strengths you believe are your highest attributes. Pray over each one and ask the Lord to guard you in each area and to bring a word of caution from His word if you begin to move into the place of ease.

Day 18

"Yet He knows the way I have taken; when he has tested me, I will emerge as pure gold. My feet have followed in His tracks; I have kept to His way and not turned aside. I have not departed from the commands of His lips; I have treasured the words of His mouth more than my daily food. . .He will certainly accomplish what he has decreed for me, and he has many more things like these in mind"

(Job 23:10-12,14).

The Lord goes before you. The path you travel, the sometimes rocky path, filled at times with falling boulders, pot holes the size of craters, are all not only traveled first by the Savior; but, the very path you at times despise, was and is created by the Lord God Almighty. God has gone before ever you were born. His eye sees every hole, the gravely spots on which you may crash, each twist and turn are etched in His mind.

The Sovereign Lord of all is not taken aback when the ground before you opens up in a chasm of grief and sorrow. God does not fret at the times when you stumble and fall. He knows the boulders crashing from the hills into the valley you cannot, for a time, escape. Each one is formed by His hand.

James admonishes us to think it not strange when we face trials. They are for a specific purpose; to develop character. Character must be tested and tried in the fires of your pathway. The route you travel is not merely not unknown by God, it is His created trek for you, His child, to walk. His hand dug the holes, placed the gravel, and named every rock and crevice. Nothing can come into the life of a child of God but that it has gone before the Throne for divine approval long before your existence.

We are the sheep. The sheep never run ahead of the Shepherd. They follow the shepherd's voice and leading. The Shepherd leads the way over hills, into valleys and over vast mountain tops. The sheep listen to the voice they know will never lead them into harm or danger but only on a path to water, lush fields in which to graze on the finest of pastures. The path may be rough and at times full of peril but the sheep are under the shepherds care.

Lord, my Shepherd, I will listen for Your voice because I know my path is known intimately to You. Your hands formed every step of my way and whatever the path may be I shall become gold along the way. Thank you Lord. Amen.

How will you listen to the voice of the Shepherd today? What are the voices that threaten to drown out His voice for you today? List the ways in which you will walk in His word.

Day 19

"Now what will you gain by traveling along the way to Egypt to drink the waters of the Nile? What will you gain by traveling along the way to Assyria to drink the waters of the Euphrates?"

(Jeremiah 2:18).

The Israelites quickly faced hardship and pain after they left the brutal life of Egypt behind. They soon viewed their miraculous deliverance as disappointment. They experienced hunger and thirst. The taste of the harsh desert settled in their nostrils. Empty bellies screamed for the food of Egypt. Tired, and now angry, eyes saw little of deliverance. Trust fled and was replaced by human reasoning. *"If only we had died by the Lord's hand in the land of Egypt, where we sat by pots of meat and ate all the bread we wanted"* (Exodus 16:3). Death with a full stomach was preferable if they could not see and touch the tangible of the world.

In truth, Egypt was a land of cruel slavery. The Israelites experienced God's wrath at the hands of their taskmasters. Assyria, an instrument of God's wrath once again, sent to turn the people back. We experience deliverance such as never before in salvation. Sadly, how often and how soon so many want to turn back to Egypt and encounter the Assyrians in their lives. Living for Christ means putting away the old, closing the door on what was once comfortable and taking the path that requires we follow Him.

The Lord declares *"You will be delivered by returning and resting; your strength will lie in quiet confidence. But you were not willing"* (Is 30:15). The life in Christ is too hard. We want the vehicles of the world, believing they will help us escape hardship and carry us swiftly to success. We are called to carry a cross as Christ. We are called to be holy as He is holy. In truth, the waters of our past are filled with death as the waters of the Nile filled with blood.

Turn your eyes ahead where Jesus bids you to follow. He knows the path. He fills your stomach with His Word, slakes your thirst with His presence and holds your hand for the journey.

Father, I commit myself to your way. I trust that though I cannot see the path ahead, it is the way I must take. I will trust today and not be afraid for I know that You above all have my life in Your most glorious care. Amen.

Where is Jesus asking you to follow Him today? What fears are holding you back? To what slavery are you tempted to return? What are your strategies to conquer?

Day 20

"So the sisters sent a message to Him" 'Lord, the one You love is sick'"

(John 11:3).

O the patient love of Jesus! How precious is the silence from Heaven as we bemoan our anguish. He does not rush to our cries of hurt and pain. When Martha and Mary sent word to Jesus that Lazarus was ill to the point of death, they believed the urgent cry would prompt the Lord to hasten to the bedside of the friend he so dearly loved. Instead, *He stayed two more days in the place where He was* (v6).

We believe that infinite love will rush to our cries of suffering. It is beyond our finite scope of understanding that the very love that died on the Cross to save us, will now *stay* and remain hushed. It is that rigorous love of the Divine that holds back the tender heart of our Savior until a more perfect work is accomplished in us. Pain, suffering, injustice, whatever we choose to name the things that come unbidden into our lives and assail our ordered existence, are the work of a love exceedingly beyond our understanding.

Jesus has more for you and me to learn than the comforts of an ordered existence. Accept that it is outside the scope of our created order to comprehend; but, forever and from eternity past, the plan God has for your life and mine. As we grow in Christ, the Father will over and over send the *Angel of Pain* to begin a work in you that only the Throne of God sees is needed that you will be blessed beyond measure.

James tells us to *think it not strange* when trials come. But, we do! Trials come, pain so intense we believe we will not survive and our response is, why is God allowing this to happen to me? O Child of God, it is not *allowed*, as some happenstance of the cruelty of the world. The Master has chosen and measured this to come and bless you. We do not choose the place or the cup by which the circumstances of our hurt come when it is from His hand, but neither must we rail against the messenger of its truth. Be patient under the wings of this Angel of Pain and you will soon hear the voice of Jesus as He comes to raise you someplace you have not been before and call you out of your grave clothes.

O Father, I do not understand this time of pain and suffering. But I know and trust the hand by which it is sent. Let me bow in reverence and worship as You finish a new work in me. Amen.

Can you identify a pain that feels unrelenting in its ferocity? What does God's word say? Write out the promises God has given you to safeguard your spirit each day.

Day 21

"The Israelites, however, were unfaithful regarding the things set apart for destruction. Achan, son of Carmi, son of Zabdi, son of Zerah, of the tribe of Judah, took some of what was set apart, and the Lord's anger burned against the Israelites"

(Joshua 7:1).

To fully understand the gravity of this passage, Joshua Chapter 7 is necessary for background. The men went to battle against Ai. Joshua was certain of victory. The men were first sent on a scouting mission to spy out the land. So confident of victory, the advice was to send up a small band of men, some two or three thousand (v3) and not to weary all the people. The smaller band went forward only to be thoroughly routed by the men of Ai. Devastated by the defeat upon the people, Joshua went before the Lord.

The Lord's answer was clear and precise (v10-12). Hidden sin got you here. Achan believed he could take some of the devoted things from the battle and hide his spoils of war under his tent. The resulting consequence of his sin cost the entire Israelite community. The men ran from Ai's hordes in fear.

Hidden sin will cause you to run in fear. You fear being found out. You fear exposure. You fear what others will think. You fear the consequences of the sin. So, like Achan, the sin is buried where you are convinced it will not be uncovered. The tools we use to hide sin are lies, subterfuge, justification of the action, and shifting blame. Sin is an outrage to God. He will not allow one of His own to hide sin. The price of hiding sin will cost those around us as well. The consequences of what we believe to be hidden will rise up and spill out. He will not allow its continuance in your life. Hidden sin will never work. It will ultimately destroy you and do harm to those around you.

The power of this chapter is immeasurable. Achan found himself imprisoned by the hidden sin. He watched as those he loved, his family, came to ruin through no fault of their own. His actions brought destruction to himself, his family, but also to the Israelite army. Tell God to come into your tent, look and see what is unpleasing to Him. Dig it up and burn it.

Lord, you see my all. I lay myself open before you, nothing hidden from your eye. Let no unclean thing or hidden sin remain. You have every right and my permission to expose anything unpleasing to you. Amen

Talk to God about what this may mean to you. Spend time before the Lord and listen to His still, small voice. Write down what He has revealed to you.

Day 22

"Now I urge you to take courage, because there will be no loss of any of your lives, but only the ship. For this night an angel of the God I belong to and serve stood by me saying, 'Don't be afraid Paul'. . .Therefore, take courage, men, because I believe God that it will be just the way it was told me"

(Acts 27:22-25).

Paul's confidence in God's plan for his life was so exact, that he was able to sleep during the storm. When chaos broke out around Paul, his words rang out to bring assurance to the men on the ship. Take courage! God told me. . . And Paul's life was so hidden in Christ that the outcome was settled as far as Paul was concerned. And so it is for us. We have the Bible, God's words to us so that we may also proclaim, God said.

Jeremiah 29:11 is an oft quoted scripture, *[F]or I know the plans I have for you"*. We quote it and then wring our hands because the truth of that scripture is not planted in our hearts. The mind may have knowledge but if it is not birthed in the heart by the Holy Spirit, the word remains stagnant, a dead seed.

The seed of God's word grows by adversity and challenge. As with Paul, the wind and storms bring life to God's promises. Take courage, we are told. Trust in Him. The challenge of trusting comes because of hurt and pain, when the clouds are so dark we cannot see the path ahead of us and the raging of the seas roll over any reserve we may have. It is in that time we learn the greatness of God and the power of His Word.

When God sends a man or woman on an errand, the rest is up to Him. We have every right to remind God that our life is in His hands as we walk any path on which we are sent by the Holy Spirit, be it mission work, raising children, in the workplace, in marriage or a day spent digging a garden. All of the risks are on God! Speak the Holy Word back to the Master and remind Him that this path is His design. Then, let the storms come, let the winds blow you to and fro, because all the risk is on your Savior. God is responsible for getting you where you are and for seeing you along the path.

Lord, there is no issue in my life at which you are surprised. Storms, waves, tears and even my fears are known to you. I trust you that this is the path for me today and that nothing may come to hinder your will as I trust in you. Thank you that your care for me is beyond my understanding but never out of your heart. Amen.

Write God a letter, list the storms you are facing. Tell God your fears regarding the storms that seem to rage unabated. End your letter with a declaration of trust in the Almighty and His Sovereign care over you.

Day 23

"O God, My God! How I search for you! How I thirst for you in this parched and weary land where there is no water. How I long to find you! How I wish I could go into your sanctuary to see your strength and glory. . . "

(Psalm 63:1-3)

A soul cannot experience the longing the Psalmist speaks of when that life is filled with the world. When the clamor of life, the hunger and thirst for things and delights of what is offered daily is once and for all quieted, stilled by a conscious decision to wait upon the Lord for His delights, then, and only then, does the heart become cognizant of thirsting for God.

Beware of digging in places that hold no water. God will not compete for our time. The gentle movement of the brook is heard by those who sit motionless at its edge. We are so preoccupied with the running and doing, that to sit by the water's edge and drink of the life-giving water is regulated to *when we have more time.* The flow of water gently surging through the open space never ceases, but neither does it jump from its designated path to follow us and bid us come quietly to drink in the richness.

The woman at the well, when once her soul-thirst was satisfied by Jesus, left her water-pot and ran to tell others. Her thirst was slaked not by the coming and going of everyday, but as she sat by the well. It is in sitting quietly, putting the things of our lives in the background that we find the glory and strength of God's Holy sanctuary. You will never have more time. Each day holds 24 hours, no more, no less. Use them to invest in what gives the most return. Spend time with God.

Father, forgive me for running so fast and hard that I barely give you a few, brief moments of my days. All my days are in your hand, freely given to me from above. Let me understand how you long to spend time with me. Amen.

List out all your activities for one day. Begin when you awaken until you go to bed. Where was your time with God? How much time did you give the Lord? Write out a commitment that you will earnestly seek the Lord each day.

Day 24

"Yes, though I walk through the valley of the shadow of death, I will fear no evil: for thou art with me; they rod and thy staff they comfort me"

(Psalm 23:4).

Each life has its own valleys and within those valleys are shadows that hover and follow, threatening to eclipse peace. We try to outrun the dark places, thinking that just around the corner is a new ray of light; some knowledge that will dispel the gloom. Or, a new book that will most certainly shatter the ceiling of silence in the valley. Running to another prayer meeting, we beg for mercy and support from others.

Stop. The Psalmist tells us that we will walk through valleys. We will certainly face shadows. Evil will appear to confront and confound. It does not matter what your valley is or what shadow follows you, God is there. His presence does not shift or change. His purpose will not be thwarted, ever.

In the darkest hours, when mind-numbing grief threatens to swallow your spirit, chew your soul only to then spit you out on a refuse heap of defeat and despair, then is the time to recognize and remember that the nameless, faceless shadow of evil can never win. You can never be separated from God's love and care. Because, the valley belongs to God, and He casts out fear.

Whatever the shadow over, around or in front, it is for our discipline and His glory. The staff of the Shepherd is there as well to bring assurance and comfort. *See, I go before you to make a way.* He will never leave you or me comfortless or alone. We are His, be it in the shadows or the sunshine. It is in the valley of shadows that we learn trust. The soul who fears, learns trust when all else is left and the heart is thrown upon the breast of the comforting Savior.

I would not know trust if I had not known fear that brought me to my knees in submission. I could not know that my God is mighty to save had I not been on the precipice of failure. I would not learn praise had I not been in the throes of despair and watched the mighty waters of my fear rise at the command of the Lord God Almighty. Like Paul, we learn rather to glory in our infirmities for it is then we learn who He is and His Glory shines through. And so, I thank Him for the valleys.

Lord, I do not understand now but I know that you are who you say you are and in that I trust without wavering. To whom shall I go but you? You alone have the words of life whether in the dark or the light, the valley or the mountain top. Thank you. Amen.

Dark places are a part of life and growth. Valleys are profoundly important if you are to learn who you are and, more vitally, who God is. List some dark places in your life right now. Tell Jesus that you will trust Him, and then tell Him why you will trust in Him even though the way seems dark.

Day 25

"God's love is meteoric, his love astronomic, His purpose titanic, his verdicts oceanic. Yet in his largeness, nothing gets lost; not a man, not a mouse, slips through the cracks"

(Ps 36:5-6, MSG)

Without a proper view of God's immense power we cannot understand His immeasurable love. God's love drives His power. And I cannot understand the great love of the Lord, the love that drove His one and only son to the cross unless and until I read His word. The Word is alive and active. It drives a spear into your soul.

We may read words on a page and be amused. Written words have the capacity to bring tears to a jaded soul. Words give direction to the lost, encouragement to the sorrowful, and laughter to the downhearted. But God's Word is more, infinitely more. When you open the Word of God for yourself, aligning your vision to the letters formed into words, and you begin to read, it is the beginning of a relationship, not a history lesson.

Life comes off the pages. Breath rises to enter into your lungs. The breath of life surges through you carrying seeds small and powerful. They are seeds of a new life. The words are kernels pulsating to bursting with sprouts of the same wisdom and power and love and life that brought the Son of God to earth to die for you. You cannot acquire this life in any way other than the Word of God. You must read it for yourself.

Hearing others speak the Word is powerful and encouraging. Spoken words whether from the pulpit or a friend can be, and often are, pathways that open up for the thirsty heart a new walk. They are God's very own words to you, to your soul and hungry heart. God longs to speak with you, personally and daily. Read His Word. Let your eyes scan the love letter God has written with His own hand. Read it over and over. Cry out for more insight, more understanding of its love and depth of knowledge that the Son has shed for you. Put your name within the verses. Read the Psalms as a letter written just for your eyes.

Father, I cannot live without your breath in me. I long to hunger for your word and yours alone above the clamor of my daily living, and the world. Thank you for your personal word to me. Amen.

Find a quiet place today and commit 15 minutes to God's Word, nothing else. No books, no quotes, no CDs on spiritual things, no preaching, just the pure milk of the Word of God. Then take some moments to write your own reflections on what you have read. Inspire yourself. Thank God for His living, active Word.

Day 26

"For unto you it is given on the behalf of Christ, not only to believe on him, but also to suffer for his sake"

(Phil 1:29).

As children of God, we learn by obedience and often obedience comes through suffering. Perfection comes through trial and error, through stumbling and falling, only to rise up and understand that it is not the way to go; and, learning that the Lord has a better plan.

Suffering brings into our lives challenges and people that on our own we would avoid because they make us angry, uneasy, and their actions hurt deeply. Christ says do not avoid such as this, but glory in that He has given us a better way.

I hate suffering. I want to avoid it and I do as much as I am able to wiggle out of all hurtful situations. But over and over again, suffering has come into my life completely out of my control. It is those times when I cry out to be delivered! I want God to swoop down and take me out of the situation. Or, better yet, take out the person through whom the suffering and hurt has come. Seldom, if ever, has that happened.

Instead, I feel the Hand of my Savior on my head, a touch of reassurance, a gentle tussle of my hair, reminding me that He *knows the way that I take and I am headed for gold* (Job 23:10). I do want to be made gold, but I still want out. I stubbornly want the situation or person removed. Too often, I want revenge, big and showy. No, the Almighty says, the thorn stays. He reminds me, my strength is perfected in weakness. I will never be left alone. I will never be forsaken. Everything I have is yours, God's word tells me, and I am humbled by the immensity of the words.

Lord, I don't think I can make it another day through this pain. The hurt weighs on my heart like a ball of iron and my chest is crushed beyond my capacity to survive. I will trust you today. Give me today. I will look to your face today. Your Word is more real to me than what my eyes see and my heart feels and you promise me that through this I will not just survive but become gold. I love you. Amen.

Every heart bears pain at times that seems unbearable. Christ came to lift that burden from you in order that you will not just survive but grow. Tell Jesus today about your sorrow. Watch as He lifts the burden. Write out in detail today the sorrow. Then write in detail God's promises to you. Tell the Lord how you trust his care for you.

Day 27

"Your dead will live; their bodies will rise. Awake and sing, you who dwell in the dust! For you will be covered with the morning dew. . .

(Is 26:19).

During the 1930s the land of the once fertile Plaines became a dust bowl. Farmers, even scientists, were ignorant of the fact that planting the same crops year after year in the same spots stripped the land of its nutrients and made dust—lots of dust. Because of their lack of knowledge and inertia, people died. The ground literally became a giant bowl of dust. Deadly dust storms blew unabated across the land, killing without mercy. The horrific dust blew across open prairies unabated. It blew with such ferocity that within minutes, unprotected people suffocated under the onslaught or were blinded by the relentless force of the dust. There was no protection.

Our bodies lie in the dust at various times in our lives. At times it may be our own ignorance that brings us to a dust bowl. Sadly, too often it is inertia. We hear no new word from heaven and so we sit, choosing instead to remain unchanged. In the early days of Salvation, everything was new and bright. Every new teaching was a sky-rocket of lights and sparkles in the sky. But as the days go on, it may appear the newness has worn off and it is back to the day to day of life.

Look for the dust piles in your life. Are you lying down when God has called you to action? Are you more content to settle into the routine and avoid anything new? New things bring learning curves. We are called out of the comfortable place in which we want to remain. The same pew. The same preaching. The same Bible teaching. The same music. If that is your bent, God will leave you in the dust of your life. But know that your body is dead. The dust will suffocate you and keep you blind.

How terrible that God would leave us in the deadly dust of our contentment. I want to be troubled. I want that God should find me in the dust, unkempt and settled, and bring the storms in to move me from the awfulness of deadly dust. I want God to awaken me from my hiding place in whatever capacity He chooses so I may not die in my dust state. I want to awake and sing as the morning dew of the power of my Holy God comes over me. Curling up in a ball and ignoring God's voice is death.

Lord, I want to live in the here and now. Raise my body up from lethargy to see your new winds blowing over me. I will rise up to life and feel the morning dew of your fresh Spirit in my life. Use your hand to sweep away my dust. Amen

What dust have you allowed to accumulate in your life? Have you sat so long that now your vision is clouded, even blind, to a new thing from God? Take some time to meditate on your vision. Have you lost sight? Are you blinded to a new vision from the Lord? List some things that are old and stale in your life. Then, list things you want to change in order that you may feel the fresh dew of the Holy Spirit.

Day 28

"Thou shalt hide them in the secret of thy presence"

(PS 31:20).

Rest assured that there is never a time when a child of God is not in the presence of the Almighty God. We may perceive that God is not there, that we are forgotten. At times our tears blind us to the holy presence. At times the choking sound of our cries keeps our head down and we cannot touch the hem of the garment. It does not mean the garment is not there, out in front of us or that it is failing to cover us in times of such desperate need.

The Israelites marched around the walls of Jericho six days. They did as directed by God but did not see any startling move. Nothing happened. They marched in obedience. They marched because they were assured of the one calling the marching orders. They trusted that His presence was there.

We cannot always see Him. We may fail to feel the hem of the garment but it does not make the reality of the covering any less. When tears blind eyes and the racking sorrow in your soul keeps your head bowed, rest in the knowledge that it is then that you are hidden in the secret of His presence.

The secret place. No one knows another's secret place with Christ. It is the place you go to curl into a ball of pain at His feet. It is the place to cry until you are sick, away from prying eyes. It is the place to go and say *I cannot make it another day.* It is the place where you may crawl onto the lap of the Savior and His arms hold tight until the horror of the hurt passes. Sometimes it is the one place of safety and security in a world that attacks relentlessly and with cruelty. It is the place of security. It is the secret place. It is the place where the nail scared hand of Jesus lifts your chin to look into His eyes and His alone until the pain passes.

Oh Lord, keep me in the secret place of your heart. It is ours and ours alone. I trust you to always have my secret place in the center of your heart. I love you. Amen.

Go to your secret place today with the Lord. Sit and experience His presence. Speak aloud His promises and affirm back to Jesus that you are taking Him at His Word. List several promises from the Lord. Speak them out loud, over and over again, in a firm and confident voice. They are truth and life.

Day 29

"I will instruct thee and teach thee in the way which thou shalt go; I will guide thee with mine eye"

(Ps 32:8).

God's plan unfolds in our lives even as the seasons come in eagerly but in their appointed time. When we are eager to know the way in which we should go, God is not deaf to the cries. He heeds every prayer and every thought as we ponder which way to go, how to do a thing and when.

It is our own impatience that hinders. Take time to wait upon God. Waiting is a lost art. Our lives have become instant everything. With the touch of a keyboard information blows up before our eyes. Food is fast and plentiful in the Drive-Thru, on the road and in microwaves at home. Hundreds of television channels are at the fingertip, offering any topic desired. We do not always have the wisdom to make good decisions instantly.

The internet supplies misinformation and gossip. It brings lies wrapped in pretty packages and people are persuaded that if it is on a screen it is true and right. Food prepared quickly and eaten on the run is seldom full of good things. Television offers up quick escapes for boredom and inertia.

Waiting on God is, and can be, hard work. Waiting on the Lord insists that I put down my own devices; the Internet, the myriad books written telling me all things I need to know about God for success and peace, the fast food of seminars and conferences, and even the best advice of friends. God alone unfolds His way and always in His time. It is our responsibility to wait.

Waiting is not inertia. Waiting is reading His Word. It is prayer. It is worship. Waiting is going about our daily lives in the knowledge of God and trusting His way beyond all else. Waiting is hearing confirmation in songs, in the words of friends and in prayer. Waiting is God's grace for each day.

Waiting in the presence of our Holy God is a privilege beyond measure. The Sovereign God of all creation bids us come and sit in the throne room. What an unspeakable honor. Don't waste it and never fail to be awed by such time.

Lord, give me grace to wait on thee. Grace to know, just as the Israelites knew that your presence was all around the walls of Jericho preparing them to fall at your command. Give me grace to walk each day in obedience and know your presence. And Father, thank you for the unspeakable honor of being with You. Amen.

Tell God today how deeply moved you are to be in His Presence. Describe being in the presence of God. Struggle with the words until you are able to put down what this is for you. Ask Him to teach you, to tell you great and glorious things about Himself.

Day 30

"Then the Lord answered Job out of the storm. He said: 'Who is this that darkens my counsel with words without knowledge?'" (Job 38:1-2) *"You have done these things, and I kept silent; you thought I was altogether like you. But I will rebuke you and lay out the case before you"*

(Ps 50:21).

Our pain takes us places we never want to go and once there, too often become trapped in tentacles that refuse to let go. Screaming and pulling we fight endlessly to escape the hurt. We fail to see the freedom of our pain. The hand of the Lord becomes obscured by the little suction cups of anger, confusion and self-pity. The vastness of wisdom reaching out to fill our hearts and minds is drowned out by our own cries.

I have over and over again screamed to heaven, *Get me out of here! Let me be free. If I were only delivered out of this pain, then my service would be richer, deeper and reach farther.* If only. Into our storm comes the voice of the Lord God. Listen. Our own words bring darkness deeper into the chasm that we see as separating us from God's love and mercy. We fail to perceive that the storm *is* the love and mercy. The dark holds wisdom beyond our finite understanding. The very grief that we curse is the knowledge we seek. Our eyes behold from an earthly point of view. And then we walk into the assumption that as we see, so God sees. God rebukes us with the truth that He is not like us. We are not like Him.

It is in the rebuke of the Lord that we become silent. Then and only then, do we sit still in our grief, our pain and anger, and come to the knowledge of who we are and that God is I AM THAT I AM. We see that the hand of the Lord is not just with us, it is His hand leading us into the storm, not around it. It is in the Tsunami we become mighty warriors in the army of the Lord.

This storm is evidence that God has entrusted me beyond my comprehension.

O Lord! I would not choose this. But I choose you. I choose to follow you, to listen to your words in the storm. I am without knowledge! Forgive my arrogance. I will sit at your feet. I will hear your rebuke and trust you. Amen.

What storms are you fighting right now? Stand back and look at this storm from God's point of view. Why is it here? Why now? Tell the Lord that you will stand still and wait His salvation. Take time today to meditate on what God would tell you right now.

Day 31

"Concerning this, I pleaded with the Lord three times to take it away from me. But He said to me, 'My grace is sufficient for you, for power is perfected in weakness'"

(II Corn 12:8-9).

Regardless what people say about grief and about time healing all wounds, the truth is there are certain sorrows that never fade away until the last breath is gasped and the heart ceases to pump blood through your body. Certain sorrows follow you as assuredly as your skin covers your body. You cannot escape them. They scream in your ear day in and day out. There may be moments of respite, during sleep, times you laugh with friends, when your mind is occupied by the needs of every day, but you know as surely as you are alive, the memory waits for a more opportune time. And at any moment, without warning, that snarling beast within the fibers of your remembrance will jump again to scream at you.

You beg and plead. You call your most trusted friends to pray and fast for you. You run to every promise of deliverance. In the darkness of the night, you fall on your knees to bargain with God, if only this thing will be taken from you. You did not ask for this! You did not cause it! Yet, it is yours to walk with its arms and legs wrapped around you like a monkey clinging to its mother for nourishment. Books, seminars, and conferences all promise the answer. They do not answer. Heaven is shut up. You believe God is silent, that He has forgotten you. Is there no mercy for me, you ask God.

But, you are bathed in the fresh mercy of the Lord. You are strong in this weakness because God has called you to a special walk with Him. This thing, whatever it be for you, is God's highest calling in your life. Others will not understand it. Those outside you will not see the call of God in this suffering. They will judge. Let them be. You are on a high calling. God's strength in weakness is His highest calling.

Father, at times feel I cannot endure another day of this sorrow. This grief swallows me into an abyss I can touch. The tears and my own crying threaten to choke me. I trust you. I believe you have heard my petitions and know the way I shall take. Let my life honor you. Amen.

Is there a sorrow in your life that seems overwhelming? Share with the Lord your sorrow. Allow His Word to comfort you, to bring unspeakable joy into this place. Affirm that you will daily walk with Him and know that nothing can separate you from the mighty love of God.

Day 32

"But seek first the kingdom of God and His righteousness and all these things will be provided for you"

(Matt 6:33).

It is seldom that these words of our Lord are taken seriously. We are certain that we must take care of our physical needs first and foremost. I must have food. I must have shelter. I must have money for my bills. I must have a job. It is the way the world works, we all believe. Jesus goes on to say, don't worry about tomorrow. There is enough worry to go around and it will be there tomorrow and the next day, and the next.

Jesus is nowhere telling us to simply let go of everything in our lives. He is telling us that in order to live to the fullest and richest as He has intended all along for us to live, we must put Him and His kingdom first. We are to seek His face daily. Immerse ourselves in God's Word for life and direction. As my children grew, I pounded into them the truth that every answer to every question is found in God's Word. Over and over I emphasized that it is impossible to come to the Lord with a dilemma or problem that has not already been answered and met by the Word. Every answer to every issue and care in this world, past, present and future is in the written Word of God. We find all that we need first and foremost as we meditate on the Word, seek His face in prayer and commit our lives to Him above all else.

To do so is not a truth that can be understood outside of the realm of believing in Jesus Christ as Lord and Savior. To aver to someone who has no relationship with Jesus or a person to whom the Savior means little or nothing makes as much sense as inviting your cat to dinner at your table and expecting to have a conversation.

When Jesus told us to seek Him first, that is exactly what He meant. First.

Lord, Sovereign King, I know and trust that every answer, every need for my life is met in You. I find You in the Word. Let me never forget nor fail to seek first and to seek diligently all that I need in Your Holy Word. Thank You for providing all that I need to live and more than I need to bless me. Amen.

What do you have need of today? Next week? Next month? Be specific. Then allow God to lead you in His word. Write down what God tells you. Read it each day and thank him for that provision.

Day 33

"God, make a fresh start in me, shape a Genesis week from the chaos of my life"

(Ps 51:10, MSG).

David's cry came from a heart filled with the anguish of recognized sin in his life. Nathan had come to David and confronted him about his sin of adultery with Bathsheba. His life was chaos; utter ruin as far as David was concerned. He had sinned against God and realized his only hope was divine mercy, more mercy than David could even imagine.

When we live outside of God's divine realm we are in chaos. When we make decisions based on our own way, confusion will reign. David had deliberately walked into a place in his life that he knew was sin. The ensuing bedlam resulted in adultery, murder and the death of an innocent child. In a short period of time, David managed to break several, if not all, of the commandments. The decision to do so was not one giant leap into the abyss; but, one led to another, and another, and another until the tiny crack became a crevasse. The fleeting thought ballooned into obsession. David became consumed with first possessing a woman married to another, followed by an attempted cover-up to hide his first sin. Finally, murder of an innocent man became, in his mind, the only viable option; until, finally, an innocent child died as a result. Chaos.

When sin enters as a result of walking outside of God's will for our lives, bedlam is the result. We may live within the disorder for a time as it quietly roils below the surface of our everyday lives. Certain we are able to deal with it, the rumblings are low in the beginning. But soon, one crack appears, a fissure opens and the ensuing pandemonium becomes the death knoll of our spiritual life and peace with God.

David believed he had hidden his sin. It is impossible to hide from God. David understood that (Psalm 139). Invite God into your chaos, whatever it may be, and cry for the same mercy that God so lavishly poured upon David. That mercy restored David and he remains "a man after God's own heart". We receive no less as we confess and throw ourselves upon the same merciful heart of our Savior.

Heavenly Father, you and you alone know my heart. I give you free and unfettered permission to enter into my secret places, expose, cleanse, use whatever means that I will be made clean and whole before you. I trust in the mercy that never runs dry. Amen.

Today write out the chaos that threatens you. Perhaps it is willful sin you chose to ignore but will not remain silent. Commit to God that you will listen to Him and Him alone as He brings peace and restores joy.

Day 34

"That they all may be one; as thou, Father, are in me, and I in thee, that they also may be one in us"

(John 17:21).

In praying for a specific thing, an answer to a need, a nod to a request, the Lord is not so much interested in the thing or our plea, as in ourselves, who we are and who we are becoming in the asking. Granting or not granting is immaterial, it is us, ourselves. God desires that we should become all in all in Him. It is of no consequence whether I get a thing or am denied the grand heavenly decision. But who am I as I pray? What is happening in my heart as a consequence for that which I pray. Does my request bring me near the throne in quiet trust and awe of the Holy Sovereignty? Am I brought near to a place of peace because I see not the thing, or the answer but I am in awe of the glory of the Lord.

My needs, my requests, my pleas then become vehicles upon which I ride to the throne of God Most High. I can say, why my God has known all the time. This has only served to reveal Him to me in a way I could never know Him elsewise.

The circumstances of a need, the people through whom the need arrives, the hurt administered, are the sign posts, the traffic lights, the curves and potholes, all leading me to the Throne. Each thing in the life of a child of God is merely a vehicle upon which we are transported to the glory and knowledge of God. Some are lemons, some jalopies, some out-right wrecks, and some pristine in their beauty. The vehicle may change, and almost certainly will, but they are all on a collision course with God.

The loneliness that wraps itself around you right now is for God's glory. Walking through times of sorrow is so that God's grace and presence might be shown in your life. We are not our own. Jesus' prayer is that we may be one with the Father. Above the fray for everyday comforts, God hears the prayer of the Son. And from heaven comes, *this rejection will produce in you patience for the coming trials; the failure you face today will show a greater way, the ones maligning you today will produce in you opportunity for my love and mercy to shine.* We belong to Jesus. He has every right to work in us all that will make us one with the Father. It is His prayer. We have no right to tell Him to leave us as we are. God will not leave us alone until we are one with the Farther. He hears the prayer of his Son.

Lord Jesus, I put my hand in yours today. Your promise is to make me as you are. I cannot see clearly right now the way of this thing in my life, but I trust in your sovereign care for me. Thank you. Amen.

Tell God, right now, that it is your desire to be one with Him. Write out your thoughts as you ponder what that will mean for your life. Is this difficult for you? What do you perceive as holding you back?

Day 35

"Though the fig tree does not bud and there is no fruit on the vines, though the olive crop fails and the fields produce no food, though there are no sheep in the pen and no cattle in the stalls, yet I will triumph in the Lord; I will rejoice in the God of my salvation!"

(Hab 3: 17-18).

Wondering where God is when we hurt is as natural as a beating heart. Do not be dismayed by your questions when you cry out that God seems far away and even appears cruel in what is allowed in your life. Shout those questions out to God. He wants to hear you and He is ready to answer. *Call upon me in your day of trouble and I will answer thee, I will tell you great and powerful things* (Ps 50:15).

Keeping silent in your pain, believing stoicism is a badge of honor will foster greater hurt and eventually turn to self-pity. Self-pity becomes a prison of one, no one comes in and no one can get out. Know that your answers are on the way. Your cries are heard in heaven and have reached the Father's ear before the last syllable leaves your lungs. The enemy may delay the answer, if the Sovereign God of Heaven so allows; but, he cannot stop God's answer and order in the life of His child. God's delays are for your good and His glory. His plan is faultless.

Cry out to heaven assured that the very atoms that make up space and time are stairs to the heavens carrying your screams unhindered to your

Heavenly Father. His answers return speedily to a waiting and trusting heart. Do not listen to the naysayers who would make excuses for what you may see as delays or no word from Heaven. They offer up excuse after excuse for God. He does not need, nor He is asking for, people to stand in his stead making excuses. He is I AM THAT I AM. Time after time, as I waited for answers from heaven, my heart breaking with the weight of what seemed unanswered prayer, my only and daily refrain became, "I know that God is who He says He is". I held to that as a life-line. It was my air hose up from the sea I believed swallowed my life. There are undeniable truths we must hold before our eyes daily; God is faithful. He is who He says He is. And the Devil is a liar out to destroy my soul. I know these because His Word tells me in no uncertain terms. From this secure place of truth, I will wait upon Him.

Jehovah, you are true and truth is found only in you. I will look up, I will watch for my answer. I will trust that not one moment is wasted. Amen.

What is swallowing you up right now? What threatens to envelope you? Tell God you know the enemy is a liar. Put all your trust in the King of Kings.

Day 36

"Rejoice always, pray without ceasing, give thanks in all circumstances; for this is the will of God in Christ Jesus for you. Do not quench the Spirit. Do not despise the words of the prophets, but test everything; hold fast to what is good; abstain from every form of evil"

(I Thes 5:16-22).

There are days when this seems an impossible task. Days when the heart is burdened with sorrow or anger, even bitterness. In the depths of a hurt so deep and intense it robs you of breath, Paul's letter to the Thessalonians seems a mockery to your spirit. How can I possibly rejoice in this? How am I able to give thanks for this circumstance? Paul has an answer for those questions. Paul, perhaps more than many, knew what it was to rejoice in all things, to give unceasing thanks, and to allow prayer to flow as a stream down a mountain.

Begin by never despising the words of the prophets in God's Word. Read them, meditate on their message in your life and circumstance. Do not quench the Spirit. In quiet allow the Holy Spirit to sweep over your circumstances. Determine to hold fast to what is good regardless of what is happening around you. You have the ability to abstain from evil. It is your choice. Make it your goal to arrive at the place where prayer is the very breath in your lungs. Get alone with God, be still in His presence. Quiet your soul and mind. This requires an act of will on our part. The quietness of time alone with God gives voice to the Holy Spirit. Being alone with the Lord opens up a window into the heart and mind of God that we find in no other way.

The Holy Spirit is alive and active in your life. Any lack of conscious awareness does not alter His movement. God is not silent. Jesus is keeping you in tune with God the Father every minute of every day. It is this knowledge that gives voice to those quick, unceasing prayers as we go throughout the day. We are not required to understand it. But we are bound to acknowledge it.

Precious Savior, I am in awe of the knowledge that your Spirit is in me, never leaving, never ceasing to intercede for me before the Throne. Let my heart sing and my lips utter praise for this every day. Amen.

Examine your time with God. Are you able to practice the unceasing prayer of which Paul speaks? Take time today to write out goals for your time alone with God. Write out steps you will take to accomplish your goals. Make a list of those for whom you wish to pray. Put dates on your list and make certain to record the answers.

Day 37

"Remember this day when you came out of Egypt, out of the place of slavery, for the Lord brought you out of here by the strength of His hand"

(Ex 13:3).

Lord, this is the day. God calls us to remember this day. He will bring us out of Egypt, free us from bondage and cruelty, out of the place of slavery. It is His promise to us. This he will do by the strength of His hand. As we leave Egypt by divine deliverance, the Lord promises to lead us to a land of milk and honey. His word is true and he cannot lie. This will be our testimony in the future –God promised by His hand and He has done it. Meditate on the circumstances of your own bondage. Define the slavery you see in your life.

As you leave this Egypt, the way may seem contrary, even frightening. God did not allow the people to travel the nearest route, maybe the most logical to them, because it was a road by the Philistines and would lead to conflict. The conflict would frighten the Israelites and their first reaction would be to return to the safety of Egypt and slavery again. Egypt was not a good place to be but it was a known enemy. The known is preferable to the unknown, even if it is bad. God knows that it is our propensity to return to the known even if it is slavery, because of our fear of the unknown.

God promises to lead a different way, a superior way. It may seem not a better way, but God has promised to be in charge of this way. And God is not a man who lies, nor the son of man who changes his mind (Numbers 23:19).

He speaks and acts on the divine promises. Our part is to trust and expect God to act.

Heavenly Father, perhaps this way or this circumstance may seem contrary to me, even disastrous; but, you know. I trust you to know my good, the best for me. Deliver me from my fears and anoint me with the courage to follow where you lead. Amen.

What is God bringing you out of today? Define the bondage you face. Write it out. Say it out loud. What path are you being shown that you have never seen before? Does it frighten you? Why? Tell the Lord?

Day 38

"The Lord then said to Moses, 'Write this down on a scroll as a reminder and recite it to Joshua: I will completely blot out the memory of Amalek under heaven'"

(Ex 17:14).

God promised to blot out the memory of the warring Amalek following a battle in which the Israelites were victorious. When Moses held up his hands, Israel won, when he grew tired his hands went down to his sides. The battle began to be lost. Hur and Aaron stood at his sides and held up his arms. God's promise to completely blot out the memory of the warring Amaleks means to remove any concern that the Amaleks would pose a threat to another nation. Israel could walk freely because God took care of the threat.

The Lord is your promise. You do not remove the memory but you blot out the threat of the enemy's ability to use that memory against us. God blots out the threat of the past and the enemy may no longer use the past as arrows to wound, taunt or threaten. Each of us has an Amalek in our lives. For some it is the agony of betrayal. It may be lies the enemy uses as swords to poke and pierce you daily. It may be the onslaught of memories of a hurt. God promises to war with those threats for as long as it takes. He enters the battle and takes over the fight.

C. S. Lewis said, "The past is frozen." How true. Begin to understand that the past has no power to come into your future, nor does the past have a voice to taunt you. It is frozen. God promised to blot out the memory of

Amalek. He will do the same for you. That memory will remain frozen, blotted out, and be powerless to chase you down. God said so. He cannot lie.

God, you are awesome in power. I believe you word is true. I am secure in your love and care for me. I will stand still and watch as you blot out the memory of the Amaleks in my life.. Amen.

What things keep taunting you? List those things from the past, whether done to you or you have done. Pray out loud and claim God's promise to blot them out. Thank him. Now take a marker and draw a line through each one. Fold up your list and put it in the freezer as a reminder that each one is frozen.

Day 39

"The angel of the Lord found her by a spring of water in the wilderness. . .She gave this name to the LORD who spoke to her; You are the God who sees me, for she said 'I have now seen the One who sees me"

(Gen 16: 7,10).

Hagar sat weeping, alone, in deep anguish. She had been sent out into the wilderness with her son. Death was the ultimate finish for her and the boy. No food, water, no shelter. Her aloneness overwhelmed her. She wept with abandon. In her deep despair, Hagar could not bear to watch her son waste away and die.

God heard this woman's desolate anguish. We are never out of the sight line of the Savior. God spoke to Hagar, what is wrong? Do not be afraid Hagar. I AM is here to provide all that you need. We may never come to the point of seeing God's abundant provision, His bounty for us unless, and until we, like Hagar, find ourselves to the point where we sit down in abject emptiness and wait bitterly.

Never be afraid to wail before the Lord. Do not spend wasted time trying to buck up in yourself when you are in a desert place and your jug of water and meager bread is gone. As our storehouse of what we call provisions, i.e., friends, books, church services, advice of others is finally depleted, then do we wander into the wilderness of Beer-Sheba, sit down alone and wait. Your place of wilderness is exactly where God is and sees you. It is His hand that has led you here because it is the place of your most plentiful provision.

God opened Hagar's eyes in the wilderness. Only when she had used up every provision of man, however meager, did Hagar have the ears to hear God call her. She left the place, sustained both she and her son, declaring The God Who Sees Me has met my need. El-Roee sees you sitting in the wilderness and He is your provision.

Father, my Savior, my provider, you alone see me in this wilderness. You alone know the anguish of my heart. I want wait upon you, empty and sorrowful. You are my comfort. Amen.

What is your wilderness today? Are your own provisions gone, used up? Tell God exactly what you need for this day. Wait upon Him for His voice, His sustenance.

Day 40

"This is what the Lord says: The wise must not boast in his wisdom; the mighty must not boast in his might; the rich must not boast in his riches. But the one who boasts should boast in this, that he understands and knows me—that I am the Lord. . ."

(Jeremiah 9:23-24).

Each day we are in a battle between what our eyes behold and what our spirit knows. As a child of God, the spirit knows that she knows God is light and in Him is no darkness. The sights and sounds around are like the disco ball, flashing light in starts and stops, luring the eye this way and that, promising delight if we will look in its direction. That is not real.

God is not of the earth and as His child you are not either. Jeremiah was told not to boast in wisdom or in physical might because what was that in comparison to understanding who God is. It is nothing. And like the strobe light, its bulb will burn out, the twist and turn of the flickering will cease.

Knowing God is supernatural and walking in the supernatural with Jesus is beyond our earthly comprehension but is more real than the ground upon which you walk. Our nature wants to grasp the unknowing and make it a physical property of understanding. It cannot be done in the spiritual. God is not like us; and yet, He became one of us. The two do not make sense in the natural. In the spiritual it is as simple and real as our own bodies in the here and now. Stop trying to make Jesus fit into your practical world and logical assumptions. We cannot do it. Once I accept that God is more than I can comprehend, His understanding inscrutable, His ways not my ways and His thoughts not my thoughts, then Jesus appears in all His glory and I see Him as I have not seen Him

He is the Lion of Judah out to fight for you. He is the Rose of Sharon to comfort for your comfort. He is the King of Kings to reign in your life. Know that He is I AM THAT I AM.

Lord, I bow to you today, to your unsearchable ways and your power to sustain me. I thank you that you are beyond my understanding. I trust in all that you are. Amen.

What are you fighting today? What circumstances have made you forget who God is? Identify those things. Write out a promise to the Lord to search Him and to wait as He reveals Himself to you.

Not The End, But A Beginning. . .

". . .[A] leader of the synagogue came in and knelt before [Jesus], saying, 'My daughter has just died; but come and lay your hand on her, and she will live.' And Jesus got up and followed him with his disciples."

(Matt 9:18-9).

The synagogue leader's daughter was not sick or even near death. She was dead. His daughter, precious to him and to his wife, was no longer alive. Her heart had ceased beating. She grew cold as only death can make the body. Her chest no longer rose and fell with oxygen moving in and out of her lungs. None of the hard facts about death and its finality apparently mattered to the girl's father. Scripture records that he came *suddenly* to where Jesus was. He burst on the scene, pushing back the crowd that surrounded Jesus. He came to the One he knew was able to raise the dead, to bring life back to his daughter. The man did not falter in his words. It was a statement of fact, not a question. *Come. Lay your hand on her. She will live. Jesus got up and followed him.* We know the scripture. Jesus took her by the hand and she got up, alive.

I can think of no other scripture more appropriate to end this 40 Day journey. This scene is not about death. It is about life. It is about Jesus wanting to call to life in you that which you see as dead. You hear no heartbeat, see no breath rising and falling in this thing, it is cold and lifeless. Come to where Jesus is for you. Rush in boldly. Declare to Jesus what is dead in you. He will come.

Finally, when Jesus arrived at the house, and declared that the girl was not dead, only sleeping, the crowd laughed. As you walk in the truth for yourself that Jesus will restore to life that which is now dead, people will wonder, not believe, not share your vision for renewed life in the particular thing. Let them. But also, ignore them. This girl's father did and he was proved right. Shake the dust off that vision. Remove the grave clothes and run with it.

—∾—

If these 40 Days have in any way enriched you and helped you to move forward in the amazing journey God has planned for you, I want to hear from you. Give me the privilege of rejoicing with you for your future and your amazing vision. I hope you will take the time to contact me at www.christineauthor9@gmail.com.

www.ingramcontent.com/pod-product-compliance
Lightning Source LLC
Chambersburg PA
CBHW030711110426
R18122000001B/R181220PG42736CBX00006B/7
9780988878136